Looking Back at
Medicine

**SCHOOLHOUSE
PRESS**

Author: Anne Mountfield

Editorial Planning: AMR

Designed and typeset by The Pen and Ink Book Company Ltd, London

Illustrations by: Jane Cheswright, Kay Dixey, Douglas Hall and Sally Launder

Picture research by: Liz Rudoff and Faith Perkins

Printed in Hong Kong

88/89/90/91/92/93   6   5   4   3   2   1

Library of Congress Cataloging-in-Publication Data.

Looking back at medicine.

Includes index.
Summary: Surveys the history of medicine, from its beginnings in ancient Egypt and Greece, through the development of hospitals and various discoveries on treating diseases, to modern developments and medicine in the future.
1. Medicine--History--Juvenile literature.
[1. Medicine--History.]
R133.5.L66 1988   610'.9   87-12504
ISBN 0-8086-1179-8
ISBN 0-8086-1186-0 (pbk.)

Photographic Credits

t=top b=bottom l=left r=right

The author and publishers wish to acknowledge, with thanks, the following photographic sources: 7, 16, 19r, 33t, (Bettmann Archive, New York), 28 (Bettmann Archive, New York) BBC Hulton Picture Library, London; contents, 11l (University of Glasgow), 11r (Courtesy of the Royal College of Physicians), 20 (City of York Art Gallery), 23l, 34 (Courtesy of Christie's) Bridgeman Art Library, London; title 6, 8, 15t, 17, 25, 27t, 29r, 31, 33b, 36t, 41t Mary Evans Picture Library, London; 4 (James Hooper Collection Watersfield), 22 Werner Forman Archive, London; 9b Fotomas Index; 29l, 38-39 Sally and Richard Greenhill; 43r Robert Harding Picture Library, London; 36b Michael Holford; 12, 13, 14, 18, 30b, 35 Mansell Collection, London; 9t, 10, 15b, 19l, 26, 32 Ann Ronan Picture Library; 23r (photograph Dr. Jeremy Burgess), 27b (photograph Hank Morgan), 37, 40 (Courtesy of St Mary's Hospital Medical School, London), 41b, 42 (photograph Larry Mulvehill), 43l (photograph Hank Morgan) Science Photo Library, London; 5, 28 Wellcome Institute Library, London; 21, 39 Zefa, UK

Cover illustration courtesy of the Mary Evans Picture Library, London.

The publishers have made every effort to trace the copyright holders, but if they have inadvertently overlooked any, they will be pleased to make the necessary arrangement at the first opportunity.

Note to the reader
In this book there are some words in the text which are printed in **bold** type. This shows that the word is listed in the glossary on page 46. The glossary gives a brief explanation of words which may be new to you.

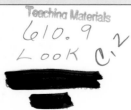

Contents

Introduction

What makes people sick? For thousands of years people have asked this question. We do not know what people thought about disease before they were able to write down their ideas.

Perhaps people knew when something they ate made them sick. Perhaps they thought their gods sent sickness to punish them. Perhaps people thought that magic or ceremonies to please their gods and goddesses would cure sicknesses.

We know that 6,000 years ago priests in Egypt studied medicine. A priest named Imhotep is said to have cured

people. After his death, he was worshipped by people as a god. His sign was a snake.

The snake sign is also linked with Moses. Moses was the leader of the **Hebrew** people. These people were later called Jews. Moses taught his people how to care for the sick. He had learned about medicine when he lived at the Egyptian court.

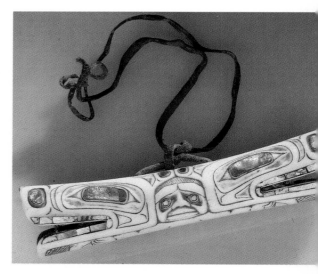

▲ This necklace is called a soul catcher. It was worn around the neck of a Native American priest-doctor. The doctor believed that evil spirits made a sick person's spirit, or soul, leave the body. The soul catcher was used to catch the soul and put it back in the body.

◀ The Greek god of medicine, Asclepius, carried a stick with a snake around it. The snake was a sign of poison and sickness. The stick was a sign of life.

About 3,000 years ago, the Greeks worshipped a god of medicine named Asclepius. People thought he would cure them if they slept all night in one of his temples. Asclepius and Imhotep are both shown in pictures with a stick. The stick has a snake wound around it. This symbol is still used as a sign for medicine today.

Early Treatments

Three thousand years ago, doctors in Egypt and Greece knew that they should use clean bandages for wounds. Also, they treated wounds with oil, wine and medicines made from plants, called **herbs**. The Greeks believed in the power of the sun, and in the need for rest. These ideas were written down. They were passed to Rome, North Africa, and **Persia**. Hundreds of years later, they reached western Europe.

Herbs have been used as a cure in India and China for more than 2,000 years. In India, doctors could operate on ears, noses and eyes. In China, doctors tried to find out how the body worked. One Chinese treatment was to stick needles in special places on the body. This stopped pain in different parts of the body. The treatment is called **acupuncture**. It is now used in many other countries besides China.

▶ Here you can see doctors at work in India. Two doctors are picking plants and flowers to make herbal medicines. Another doctor is holding a cup of medicine. The fourth doctor is taking the patient's pulse. The picture is more than 450 years old.

Medicine through the Ages

Thousands of years ago, doctors found treatments that cured their patients. Doctors today are still trying to find out why these cures worked.

In this book, you will read about how doctors and nurses have come to understand the causes of many diseases. Many cures have been found. There are still some diseases that doctors do not understand. Cures for these may be found in the future.

Early Medicine

About 2,500 years ago, Greek doctors' ideas began to change. They thought about sickness, or **disease**, and how to heal people. They wondered why things happened. They looked at the world around them in different ways. They tried to find out why people became sick.

The Greeks no longer thought that sickness was a punishment sent from the gods. They thought that sickness might be caused by something **natural**, that is, by something in the world. They watched sick people very carefully, and they wrote about the disease. This careful way of looking at disease made curing people into a **science**.

The Greeks also thought that it was important to keep healthy. They wanted to prevent sickness. They were careful about what they ate, and they got plenty of exercise.

The "Father of Medicine"

About 2,500 years ago, a Greek doctor named Hippocrates thought there must be a reason why people became sick. He decided that the gods were not to blame. He taught student doctors to study their patients with care, and to write about each person's illness. He told them to treat patients with kindness. He also told the students to regard as a secret anything that patients told them. These ideas were written down. That is how we know about them today.

▲ Hippocrates was called the "father of medicine." He was a Greek who had studied medicine in Egypt. His writings were used for many centuries by doctors.

Hippocrates became known as the "father of medicine." Today, many new doctors take the **Hippocratic oath**. They say they will always help the sick and try to treat them gently and carefully.

Galen

Claudius Galen was a Greek doctor who lived about 600 years after Hippocrates. His father had a dream that the god Asclepius wanted young Galen to study medicine. Galen studied medicine in Egypt, and also visited many of the temples of healing in Greece. Galen was interested in how the human body worked. He learned more about the body by treating wounds.

Galen went to work in Rome. He was not allowed to study the insides of human bodies. This is called **dissection**. However, he did dissect many animals, even an elephant! Galen saw that bodies have tubes full of blood. He believed that the body held four kinds of fluids. Two were blood, and spit which is called **phlegm**. There was also black **bile** and yellow bile. These fluids were called the four **humors**. Galen decided that sickness was caused when people had too much of one humor. So his cures were to let out blood, to make people vomit, or to make them empty their **bowels**. This became the chief way to treat the sick for the next thousand years. We know about Galen's cures because he wrote them down. He followed Hippocrates' way of writing down how he treated each patient.

▼ Galen became one of the most famous doctors in Rome. Here, you can see him with some of his students.

The Herb Doctor

For thousands of years, people have used plants to make medicines. We know this from writings and from pictures. One man who used herbs was a Greek doctor. He was named Dioscorides. He was a doctor in the army of the Roman Emperor, Nero. As Dioscorides traveled with the Roman army, he wrote about the plants he found and used. His book about herbs is called the *Herbarium*. It tells about plants, and the diseases they may cure. This book was used by doctors for about 1,600 years. Many people still use herbal medicines today.

▼ Dioscorides was famous for his study of herbs. He is shown on the right-hand side of this book on plants and herbs.

The First Hospitals

Greek hospitals were first built near temples. Here, priests and their helpers could take care of the sick. Their temple hospitals were called *asclepeia*, after the name of their god of medicine, Asclepius.

The Greeks believed that exercise was good for a person's health. They often built sports centers with running tracks for their patients. The remains of these hospitals have been found with ruined Greek temples. The Romans copied this idea of the hospital from the Greeks. In Pompeii in Italy, there are ruins of these Roman hospitals. They are almost 2,000 years old.

Arab Hospitals

The people of the Middle East were very interested in studying medicine. Many famous doctors came from that part of the world. Long before there were places in western Europe for sick people to be cared for, the Arabs had hospitals. In these hospitals, all sorts of cures were used that were not known in Europe. One of these was to put casts on broken bones to keep them from moving while they heal. The Arabs also studied diseases, such as **smallpox**, very closely. Also, they took care of people who were mentally ill long before anyone did in Europe.

People from Europe first saw the Arab hospitals when they went to the Middle East to fight in the Crusades. The Crusades were holy wars fought between European Christians and the people of Turkey, who were Muslims. The Turks had taken over the city of Jerusalem and the Europeans went there to free it. The Crusades went on for a long time. There were many injured and sick people. The Europeans soon used the idea of the Arab hospitals. Groups of special soldier-monks were formed. They made it their special job to nurse the sick and wounded during the Crusades. Two of these groups were the Knights of St. John and the Knights Hospitallers.

▼ These soldier-monks are Knights of St. John. They went on to battlefields to care for wounded soldiers.

Hospitals in Europe

When the people returned from the Crusades, they brought the idea of hospitals with them. The first hospitals in Europe were run by nuns and monks. This is because it was their religious duty to take care of people. The oldest hospital in Europe is in Paris. It is called the "Hôtel de Dieu." This means "God's Inn" in French. Another very old hospital is St. Bartholomew's in London. It was started by monks more than 600 years ago.

At about this time, people in Europe were able to study the ideas of the Greek and Arab doctors. Many of the Arab books were in Toledo, in Spain. They were brought there when the Arabs took over the city. These books were translated into Latin and the monks, who could read Latin, were able to use them. Other books were written from the Arab books and they had pictures which showed how patients should be treated.

In these early hospitals, "curing" patients did not always mean making them better. It usually meant taking care of them while they were sick by washing, feeding, and comforting them. Doctors used herbs to make medicines. They also studied the stars for the right times to treat their patients.

Sometimes, doctors would "bleed" their patients. This means to cut the patients to make them bleed on purpose.

▶ This Italian patient has his friends around his bedside. The doctors in the front are preparing to treat his leg.

Doctors did this because of Galen's ideas about the four humors. They thought that letting out some blood would make patients better. It often killed people, instead. Doctors also used a kind of slug called a **leech** to suck blood from patients. Early doctors were sometimes called leeches because of this.

▲ These nuns are caring for the sick in the Hôtel de Dieu, in Paris. At the bottom of the picture, nuns are sewing the bodies of the dead into sheets to get them ready for burial.

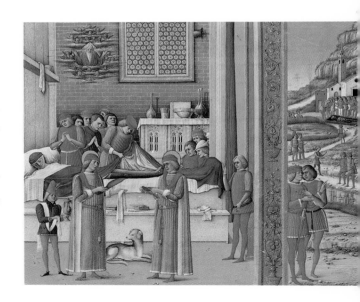

Finding Out about the Body

About 500 years ago, schools for doctors were set up in Europe. In the cities, there were hospitals where students could go to study sick people. Artists began to make drawings of the body for doctors to study. Doctors began to find out more about how the body works. They began to wonder if the teachings of Galen and others were correct. One teacher shocked people by burning Galen's books. This man's name was Paracelsus. He was Swiss. He taught at the University of Basel. He said that Galen was wrong. Paracelsus taught his students that doctors must learn from patients, not just from books.

Vesalius

Four hundred years ago, a young doctor began to teach students in Padua, Italy. His name was Vesalius. He and his students dissected human bodies. They needed to do this to learn how our bodies work. Vesalius also taught the students that Galen's ideas about the body were wrong.

Vesalius wrote a book about the human body. It was published in 1543. There were fine drawings in it. They were made by Jan Stefan van Kalkar. People who had never seen inside real bodies before, looked at the pictures. These drawings showed how the body works. People could also read about Vesalius' ideas. Vesalius became very famous.

Vesalius' work changed the way in which students were taught. Today, all medical students learn how the body works by watching bodies being dissected. Students are now able to dissect bodies themselves, too.

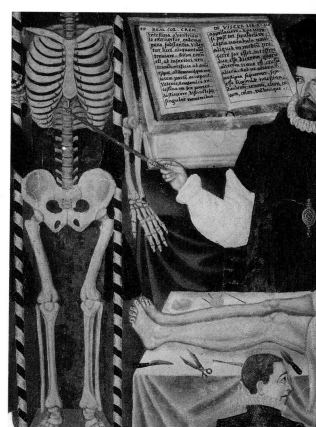

William Harvey

William Harvey was an English medical student. He studied in Padua shortly after Vesalius' time. Harvey was interested in blood. Galen had written about two kinds of tubes which carried blood. The **arteries** carried bright red blood. The **veins** carried purple blood. Galen taught that these two bloods were not linked. He thought the heart was a machine that warmed the blood. When the blood became too hot, it caused fevers. The cure for a fever was to open the vein to let out the hot blood. This would then cool the body.

◀ This picture of Vesalius was drawn by his friend, Jan Stefan van Kalkar. Vesalius is showing how the muscles of the arm and the hand work.

Harvey learned that Galen was wrong. When he went back to Britain, he cut up a heart. He saw that it was a pump. The arteries carried fresh blood away from the heart. The veins carried the blood back to the heart. The blood went around the body in a circle. Harvey guessed that there must be a link between arteries and veins. He could not see the links, but he was right. They are there; but they are so tiny, that they cannot be seen without a microscope.

In 1628, Harvey published a book that showed why Galen was wrong. Some doctors began to believe him. However, many doctors still did not learn about these new ideas.

▲ William Harvey is seen here with King Charles I of England. He is explaining that the heart pumps blood around the body. The people on the right are discussing his ideas.

◀ Vesalius' ideas spread across Europe. This is John Bannister, an English doctor, teaching his students about anatomy, or the study of the human body. They were among the first students to study the inside of a human body.

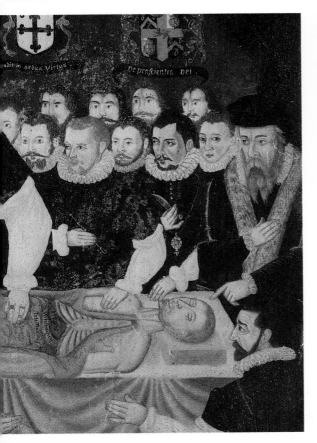

Early Knowledge of Disease

Until 300 years ago, most medical schools only taught students how the body worked. They taught students how to cool a fever and how to repair broken bones. The schools did not teach about disease. However, no one knew yet what caused disease. Some people thought that doing something bad caused disease. Some people thought bad blood was the cause. Other people thought disease was caused by bad smells, called **miasmas**.

Some diseases are caused by not having the right food. **Scurvy**, for example, is caused by not eating enough fresh fruit and vegetables. It makes the gums bleed and the bones soften. Other diseases spread easily from one person to another. These are called **epidemic** diseases.

Epidemic Diseases

When people lived closely together and their houses and water supplies were often dirty, diseases spread easily. A **plague** is a disease which spreads from rats to fleas. When the infected fleas bite people, they catch the disease. Between 1368 and 1370, half of the people in Europe died from a plague known as the "Black Death." In 1665, the plague killed about 60,000 people in London. Houses were shut up and crosses were put on the doors. This was to show that people in those houses had the plague. Many people thought the disease was a

punishment from God. When the Great Fire of London stopped the plague, they thanked God. They did not know that the fire had killed off all the rats.

Another epidemic disease is **leprosy**. People with this disease are called lepers. They must keep away from other people. In the past, lepers had to call out "unclean, unclean" when approaching people who were well. Sometimes, they had to wear a bell so that people could hear them coming. The monks and nuns who cared for the lepers often risked their own lives. If they caught leprosy, they could die, too.

◄ This is how doctors dressed 300 years ago to avoid catching the plague. The nose of the doctor's mask was stuffed with herbs to keep out smells. People believed that bad smells could give them the plague.

New Discoveries

When people knew how the body worked, they began to study each part closely. The doctors wanted to see what happened when the body was diseased. They needed something to help them to see tiny parts of the body. An instrument called a **microscope** made things look bigger. After about 1660, better microscopes were made. The invention of the microscope was a great help. Now, doctors knew that Harvey had been right about arteries and veins being connected. They could see the links between arteries and veins called **capillaries**. They could also see tiny living creatures called **microbes**. The first man to find out about microbes was a Dutchman. His name was Anton van Leeuwenhoek. Being able to see and study microbes was the first step in learning to cure disease.

◄ In London, during the plague of 1665, the bodies of the people who had died were collected at night and put into a cart. During the day, houses with plague victims were locked from the outside. The sick people were kept inside. This was to stop the spread of disease.

▼ The microscope invented by Leeuwenhoek worked like a magnifying glass. A person held it up to the eye and looked at the object from the other side.

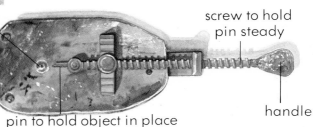

lens

screw to hold pin steady

pin to hold object in place

handle

What Causes Disease?

Today, we know that many diseases are caused by microbes known as **germs**. Germs are so small that we cannot see them without a microscope. They live and grow in our body. When we feel sick, it is because our bodies are being attacked by germs. Until about 150 years ago, doctors thought that germs were the *result* of diseases. They did not know that they caused diseases.

Jenner and Smallpox

Smallpox was one of the diseases that scared people most. About 300 years ago, smallpox killed many people in Europe. In Turkey, doctors knew that no one caught smallpox twice. If they did not die from it, they never caught it again. Therefore, Turkish doctors tried to give their patients a mild attack of the disease. They squeezed the sticky liquid out of the smallpox blisters from a person with the disease. Then, they scratched the arm of a healthy person. They rubbed the smallpox fluid into the scratch. A British traveler, Lady Mary Wortley Montagu, let Turkish doctors treat her children in this way. She felt that British doctors should try the same idea. They did not because they were afraid that their patients might die.

A British doctor named Edward Jenner found out how to prevent smallpox in a safer way. There is a mild disease called **cowpox** which is caught from cows. Jenner knew that anyone who had had cowpox never caught smallpox. In 1796, Jenner heard of a milkmaid who had cowpox. He injected fluid from a blister on her hand into a small boy named James Phipps. James caught cowpox, but he was not very sick. Then, Jenner injected the boy with smallpox. James did not catch the disease. Jenner's new treatment was called **vaccination**. Other doctors started to use vaccinations to prevent smallpox. By 1804, 12,000 people had been vaccinated. As a result, fewer people died from smallpox. Today, smallpox is no longer a killer disease. It does not exist, thanks to Edward Jenner.

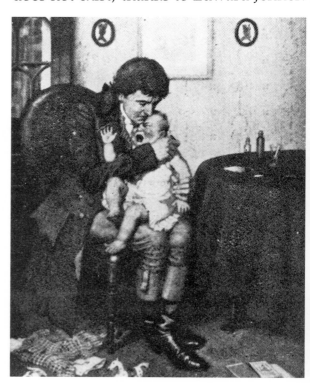

▲ Edward Jenner is vaccinating his own son against smallpox.

Pasteur

Jenner did not know what caused smallpox. A French scientist, Louis Pasteur, was the first man who showed what caused many diseases.

Pasteur had seen the microbes that lived in beer, wine and milk. He found out that heat would kill the microbes. He heated some milk and then cooled it quickly. Children who drank this milk did not become sick. Pasteur wondered why killing the microbes seemed to prevent disease. He guessed that the microbes were the cause, not the result, of disease. He called them germs. At first, no one believed Pasteur's ideas. Then, slowly, people began to believe that he was right.

▲ Here you can see Louis Pasteur studying germs through a microscope. Pasteur worked for many years in his laboratory in Paris.

▼ In this picture from France, people are being given free vaccinations against smallpox. It is likely that the artist put the cow in to remind us that cowpox prevents smallpox.

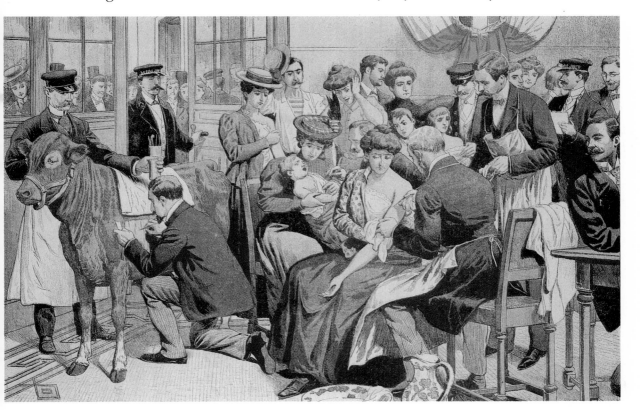

Early Doctors

A "doctor" is someone who has studied at a college or university. There are doctors of history, or of law, or of many other subjects.

The first time the word "doctor" was used to mean a doctor of medicine was 900 years ago. In Italy, the University of Salerno began to teach medicine. The students had to pass tests to show what they had learned. Then, they were given the title "Doctor of Medicine."

▼ Quack doctors said that their medicines could cure many diseases. This famous quack, Dr. Perkins, made a lot of money before people realized that his "cure" did not work.

Doctors' Colleges

About 500 years ago, many colleges were set up to train new doctors. One of the oldest is Britain's Royal College of Physicians. It was set up in London in 1518. No one was allowed to work as a doctor in London unless the College said he could. In other parts of the world, doctors remained untrained for a very long time.

About 150 years ago, many other countries began to make laws that all doctors must be trained. Lists of trained doctors were made. In the United States, a person can be a doctor only in the state in which he or she has trained. If a doctor wants to work in another state, he or she must take the exams for that state before they are allowed to work.

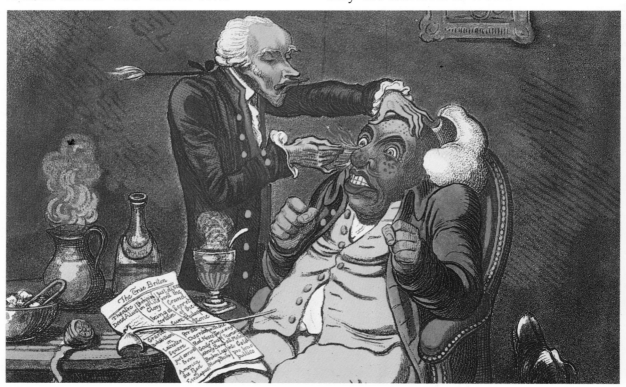

Physicians

The word "physician" was used to mean a trained doctor of medicine. The word comes from a Greek word meaning "healer."

Four hundred years ago, physicians often wore special clothes. In Britain, they wore long red gowns with wide sleeves and a small red cap. They charged a lot of money to visit a patient. Most people could not afford a physician. Most people knew more about herbal medicines than people do today. If people wanted a special cure, they often went to a "wise woman." People often thought that these wise women might be witches. They were probably just people who knew about healing.

▼ Doctors visited people in their homes to try to find out why they were sick. When this picture was drawn, in the early 1800's doctors did not have many good medicines.

Sometimes, sick people were cheated by people who pretended to be doctors. They were called quacks. Quacks traveled around the country, and sold cures that did not work. Their "wonder medicines" were usually only colored water.

▲ The British Medical Association and the American Medical Association badges are nationally recognized. They both have symbols used by Asclepius, the stick with the snake.

Famous Doctors

Some doctors are well-known for making new discoveries. There are also doctors who have been remembered for other reasons. Some did special work or were the first to do some special thing.

Father Damien

About a hundred years ago, leprosy was still a fairly common disease. There was still no cure for it. People with leprosy were called lepers. In the Pacific Ocean was a group of islands. It was the practice in the islands to send lepers to live on an island called Molokai.

▲ Father Damien was often angry with governments because they did not give him enough money. He was never angry with the lepers. He lived and died with them.

Father Damien was a Belgian monk. He felt that he should go to take care of the lepers on Molokai. In 1873, he sailed to this island. He knew he could not live there for long without catching leprosy himself. Father Damien lived on Molokai for sixteen years. He helped the lepers a great deal. Often, he got angry when lepers were sent to the island without proper food or medical supplies.

When Father Damien was forty-nine years old, he did die of leprosy. After his death, people raised a lot of money in his memory. They set up the Damien Institute, which worked to find a cure for leprosy. Drugs have now been found to cure the disease. In some countries people do not have the money to buy the medicine they need. In these places, many people still die of leprosy.

Two Women Doctors

Seven hundred years ago, there were women **surgeons** in Europe and Asia. When colleges were set up, women were not allowed to go to them. Then, only men became doctors.

One of the most important early woman doctors is Elizabeth Blackwell. When she was seventeen, Elizabeth and her two sisters started a school to earn money to look after their mother and younger brothers.

▶ These are some of the first women medical students. They are watching an operation in the Royal Free Hospital in London, in 1895. The women without caps are the medical students. The women with caps are the nurses.

In the 1840's, Elizabeth Blackwell decided to become a doctor even though her friends thought that it was a bad idea. After several years, she persuaded a medical school to take her as a student. She qualified as a doctor and went to England. The doctors in England showed her around hospitals all over the country.

Elizabeth Blackwell decided she wanted to learn more about treating women's illnesses. She had worked in Paris but caught a disease from a patient and became blind in one eye. At the same time, Elizabeth Blackwell's sister, Emily, was studying to be a doctor in the United States. In the 1850's, the two sisters opened a hospital for women in New York State. Many people thought that this was not a good idea. The Blackwells were helped by a group of people called Quakers.

▲ Elizabeth Blackwell became a doctor in 1849. Her work helped other women to become doctors.

Elizabeth Blackwell went back to London. There, in 1858, she gave a talk about the need for women doctors. In the audience was a woman called Elizabeth Garrett-Anderson. She agreed with everything that Elizabeth Blackwell had said.

Elizabeth Garrett-Anderson could not get any school of medicine to take her. She still studied to be a doctor by paying to take lessons at a hospital, but she was not allowed to take her exams. At last in 1865, she passed an exam that allowed her to mix medicines. She found that she could train in France. In 1870, she became a doctor. A hospital for women was named after her in London.

Preparing Medicines

Very early medicines had links with magic. People believed that they could cure their bodies by eating parts of animals. Many medicines were made from strange things like spiders, and worms.

▲ Here are some of the first druggists at work. They are grinding powders and heating liquids. Some druggists tried to create a medicine that would make people live forever. They did not succeed, but they learned a great deal that helped later scientists.

People who made medicines used to be called **apothecaries**. The word means "someone who keeps a storehouse." Apothecaries kept stores of healing plants called herbs. They ground the herbs into powder. Then they mixed the powder with honey and spices to make it taste better. Often, apothecaries had their own herb gardens.

Apothecaries did not always know the dangers of some plants. The drug **opium** comes from a type of poppy. For hundreds of years, it was given to stop the pain of a toothache. It was even given to babies to keep them from crying. No one knew that opium was very dangerous.

Until about 900 years ago, apothecaries and doctors were really doing the same work. Then, the doctors began to feel that they were more specially trained than apothecaries. The apothecaries did not want to be thought of as shopkeepers. They said they had special skills, too.

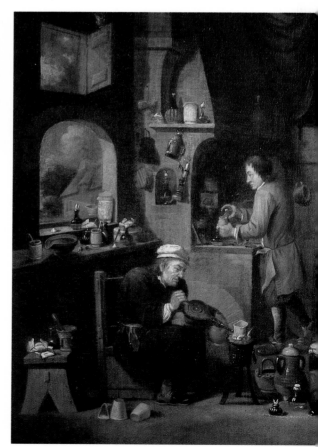

Safety in Medicine

Some plants, such as deadly nightshade, are poisonous. In many countries, only apothecaries kept and sold dangerous drugs or poisons. This was for public safety. It led to new fears. People wanted to be sure that poisons did not get mixed into the medicines. The apothecaries' shops were inspected. They had to prove that there were not harmful things in their medicines.

▼ In this Dutch apothecary's shop, there are many jars of medicine. The apothecary is heating a mixture over a burner. He is using a bellows to make the fire blaze. The recipe book for the medicine is open on the table.

Later, apothecaries had to study and pass special tests. Today, people who make medicines have special training. They are called **pharmacists**.

Today, if you need a mild medicine, like aspirin, you can buy it at a drugstore. Stronger medicines cannot be sold without a note from a doctor. This note is called a **prescription**. Sometimes, the druggist makes the medicines right in his or her drugstore. Today, many medicines are made by chemists in **laboratories**, however.

Making medicines has become a very big industry. Some companies sell their medicines all over the world. They spend millions of dollars to find new drugs to treat diseases. All new drugs are tested before they are sold.

▲ Today, hospitals all over the world use large supplies of drugs. Sometimes, these are made by druggists in the hospital laboratories. Sometimes, they are made in factories and sold around the world.

Operations

Sometimes, a part of the body becomes diseased. If it cannot be cured, it may have to be removed. The body is cut open and the part is taken out. Then, the opening is stitched up. If it is an arm or a leg which is diseased, it may have to be cut off, or **amputated**. In the past, operations were very painful for the patients. They were also very risky.

Very long ago, priest-doctors had helpers who operated on people. These helpers were some of the first surgeons. They were not allowed to call themselves doctors.

Today, all surgeons have to train as doctors first. Then, they train further to become surgeons. They can specialize in different kinds of surgery.

Early Operations

People have always needed simple operations. Boils had to be cut open. Thorns or arrow heads had to be taken out of the skin. This was first done with sharp stones.

Very old skulls have been found that show signs of a strange operation. A hole was made in the top of the head with a very sharp stone. It may have been a way to let out pain or evil spirits. The operation is called **trepanning**. We know that people lived after this operation because the skulls show that the bone has grown again.

▲ This ancient skull was found on the northwest coast of the United States, and is almost 2,000 years old. The two circular holes in the top show that the patient was trepanned twice.

About 2,000 years ago, Roman surgeons learned how to do many difficult operations. Julius Caesar is said to have been born by an operation on his mother's stomach. This type of operation is still needed for some births. It is called a **Caesarean section**, after Julius Caesar.

Thousands of years ago, surgeons in India knew how to rebuild noses. This type of operation is now done by doctors called "plastic" surgeons.

Some barber shops have a striped red and white pole outside. Long ago, it was a sign that the barber was also a surgeon. Barbers cut people's arms to let out blood. They also pulled out teeth.

Ambroise Paré was a French army surgeon. He worked at the Hôtel de Dieu in Paris before he joined the army in 1536. Paré used old Greek ways when he treated gunshot wounds. He put soothing liquids and bandages on the wounds. The soldiers got better faster. They suffered less pain than when their wounds were treated with hot oil.

Paré made notes about the amputations he had to do. He wrote several books about surgery. Other surgeons read his books. They started to change their ways of operating. Paré also made a metal hand. It had joints in it, and it could hold a pen. People who had lost a hand could be helped by Paré's invention.

▲ Over 700 years ago, surgeons treated patients with wounds and broken bones.

Ambroise Paré

Five hundred years ago, people began to use guns in battles. Guns could wound soldiers very badly. Often, soldiers had to have a wounded arm or leg cut off. These operations were very painful. Patients were held down while the limb was removed. Sometimes, they were given a piece of leather to bite on, so they did not bite their lips or tongue. Then, boiling oil was poured on the wound. This was to kill germs that might get into the wound.

▲ Ambroise Paré used egg yolk, oil of roses, and turpentine to dress wounds. This worked better than hot oil. It also hurt less.

Preventing Pain

The Greeks knew how to put patients to sleep before operations. They gave them a mixture of opium and herbs. Sleeping mixtures like these were used for thousands of years. Some were drinks. Some were herbs to sniff. Sometimes, surgeons even tried to prevent pain by making their patients drunk.

Two hundred years ago, Franz Mesmer amazed people in Paris. He sent his patients into a kind of sleep just by talking to them. While they were asleep, they felt no pain. This is now called **hypnosis**. At the time, people thought Mesmer was a quack.

One hundred years later, surgeons had become very skilful. They could do short operations inside the body. They knew how to do longer operations, but if they tried, their patients usually died. The patients could not stand the **shock** from the pain.

The New Painkillers

About 150 years ago, scientists were learning about new gases. In Britain, a scientist named Humphrey Davy suggested using gas in operations. This gas was called **nitrous oxide**. It made people feel sleepy. Another scientist named Michael Faraday tested a liquid called **ether**. He found that breathing in ether put people to sleep.

In 1831, an American chemist named Samuel Guthrie made a new drug called **chloroform**. He called it "sweet whisky." This drug made people feel drunk, and then put them to sleep.

At first, doctors did not show much interest in these new ideas. Then, in 1842, an American doctor, Crawford Long, used ether on a patient to put him to sleep. The patient did well, but news of the operation did not spread quickly.

▼ This patient has been given rum to drink before his operation. Even so, he must be held down by three strong men.

Four years later, newspaper reports made three operations very famous. The first was the work of an American dentist, William Morton. He pulled out a tooth after giving a patient ether. Then, James Warren, a surgeon in Boston, Massachusetts, used ether for an operation on a patient's neck. Before the end of 1846, a British surgeon, Robert Liston, had tried ether. Surgeons began to realize that they had a new way to prevent pain. It was called an **anaesthetic**.

James Simpson

Doctor James Simpson was a young surgeon in Scotland. He had seen his patients' fear of pain. He had also heard that ether made patients sick. Therefore, he and two friends decided to try the new drug, called chloroform. They tested it first on themselves. All three doctors fell fast asleep! When Simpson woke up, he did more tests and was pleased by the results. After that, he used chloroform during surgery. Queen Victoria was given the drug in 1857 when she gave birth to her eighth child.

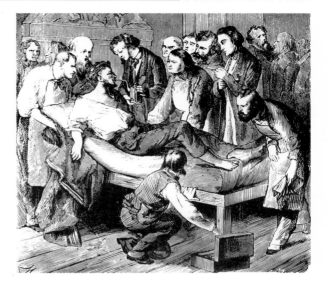

▲ There were many people who wanted to watch as this patient was given ether. The patient is breathing the ether from a jar that has a tube going to his mouth. It was difficult to give the right amount. If the doctor did not give the patient enough, he might wake up. If the doctor gave him too much, the patient could die.

▼ James Simpson, on the left, is waking up after trying chloroform. In the middle his friend, Dr. Duncan, is asleep under a chair. His other friend, Dr. Keith, is on the right.

Killing Germs

Even after a painless operation, there were still dangers for patients. Sometimes, a patient's wound became infected. Then, poison from the wound would get into the blood. The patient would become sick with a high fever. This is called **sepsis**. Many patients died from this. One question puzzled surgeons. Why did a broken arm or leg cause sepsis only when the skin was torn? Wounds inside the body did not seem to cause sepsis.

Joseph Lister

In 1865, Joseph Lister was working as a surgeon. He knew that Louis Pasteur had said that germs in the air caused diseases. Lister thought that germs in the air also caused sepsis in wounds. If this were true, then doctors should kill the germs before they could reach the wounds.

Lister began to wash all his surgical tools in a liquid called **carbolic acid**. He sprayed the carbolic acid in his operating room. He and his nurses washed their hands before they touched their patients. Then, Lister kept the air away from the patient's wounds. He covered the wounds with clean bandages. Most doctors said he was crazy to spray acid at germs he could not even see.

After a while, people found that there were fewer deaths in Lister's hospital. Other surgeons began to think that he was right. They began to copy Lister's methods. Today, surgeons wear germ-free clothes. They wear gloves and masks and operate in especially clean rooms.

Robert Koch

Robert Koch was a German doctor and scientist. He continued Pasteur's work on germs. Pasteur had found that microbes caused sickness, but he did not know which microbes caused which diseases. Koch found a way of showing which microbes caused wounds to become infected.

▲ Joseph Lister knew that germs and dirt led to many deaths after surgery. He said that an operating table was a more dangerous place than a battlefield. Lister spent twelve years persuading other doctors to try his method of killing germs with carbolic acid.

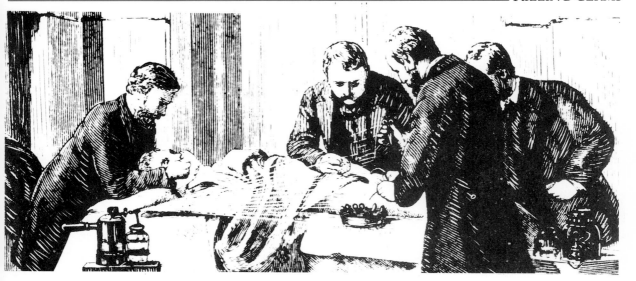

In 1881, Koch began to work on a disease of the lungs that killed most people who caught it. It was called **tuberculosis**, or TB.

In 1882, Koch found the germ that caused TB. It lived in cattle and was found in milk. Cows were soon tested for TB, and milk was **pasteurized**. TB patients were taken care of away from other people to keep the disease from spreading.

Robert Koch's way of finding the TB germ was used by many other scientists. Now, they knew how to look for a specific germ. They could find out which germ caused which disease. Then, they started to make vaccines which would prevent people from catching the diseases.

Today, there are vaccines against TB and many other diseases. However, people still die from TB, especially in places where they cannot afford to pay for the vaccine.

▲ This surgeon is using one of Lister's carbolic sprays to kill germs near the operating table. The table is covered with a clean white cloth but the doctors are still wearing their everyday clothes, and they are not wearing gloves.

▼ These modern surgeons are wearing masks and long gowns that are germ free. They are operating on a heart. It is important to keep germs out of the open body.

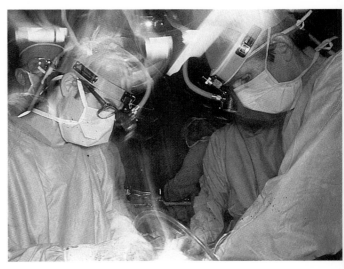

Nurses

In Egypt and Greece, sick people came to the temples to be healed. The priests had workers who helped sick people who came to pray for health. They also washed them and fed them. Many of these early nurses were slaves. This meant that they belonged to the temple. They did not get paid for their work. We know from the Bible that the Hebrews of ancient Israel had women nurses who helped at births. They were called **midwives**. For many years, nurses did not go to school to be trained. They learned from each other how to take care of the sick.

◀ "Wise women" like this one were the chief doctors of poor people for many years. This woman's herbal medicine will help to soothe the pain of the men's broken limbs.

Nuns and Monks

For hundreds of years, nursing was linked with religion. Nuns and monks gave food and a bed to any traveler on a journey. Often, travelers became sick and were nursed by these religious people. They gave them a welcome, or **hospitality**. Nuns are called "sisters." In some countries, the woman nurse in charge of a hospital ward is still called a "sister."

Nearly 1,000 years ago, there were nursing monks in the city of Jerusalem. They looked after Christian travelers. Their hospital was called the Hospital of St. John of Jerusalem. In 1099, during the Crusades, there was a battle to free the city from the Turks. Christian soldiers from all over Europe fought in this battle. The monks cared for the wounded soldiers. In return, they were given money to found Hospitals of St. John in Europe. Many other groups of monks and also nuns began to set up hospitals. Some took care of the blind. Some took care of people with leprosy. Others took care of people who were mentally ill. Hospitals also sheltered people who caught the plague. They helped the wounded, too. They took care of the sick, the old and the dying.

Standards of Nursing

Hospitals have not always been clean, safe places where sick people go to get better. About 400 years ago, in Britain, all the hospitals that had been run by monks and nuns were closed. After this happened, some hospitals became places for keeping the homeless or beggars. These places were often crowded and dirty. In 1783, one hospital was told to use "six bug traps in every ward." The nurses did not do much more than keep patients clean and feed them. No one wanted to work as a nurse. The only people who would do the work were those who could find no other job. Then, about 200 years ago, a German named Pastor Fliedner decided that something must be done. Pastor Fliedner and his wife opened three schools just for training nurses.

Today, women and men are carefully trained as nurses. They go to a school or hospital for their training. They must pass exams and spend time looking after sick people in the hospital. Then, they are registered as nurses.

▶ During World War I, from 1914 to 1918, nurses took care of the wounded soldiers. Here, they are nursing soldiers at a medical center in Poitiers, France.

▼ This American nurse is working in a hospital. It is clean and comfortable. The nurse is helping a patient take her medicine.

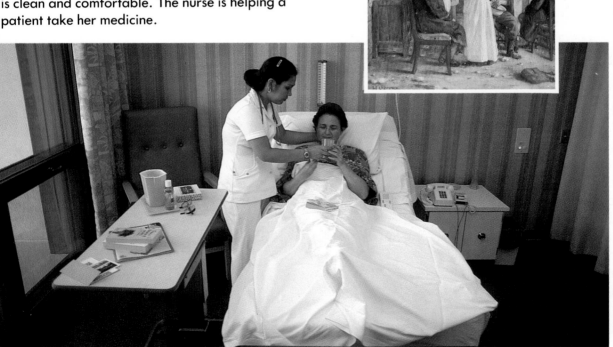

Famous Nurses

More than 300 years ago, a French girl named Jeanne Mance set out for Canada. The ship she sailed in carried French soldiers. When they became sick, Jeanne nursed them. When she arrived in Montreal, Jeanne opened a hospital for soldiers.

At that time, France owned parts of Canada. French soldiers there were fighting the Iroquois people who lived near Montreal. The Iroquois attacked the city. Jeanne had to leave her hospital in ruins. She worked for years to raise enough money to rebuild the hospital. In time, she did. Jeanne Mance's hospital is now part of the University of Montreal.

Elizabeth Fry and Dorothea Dix

In the early 1800's, Elizabeth Fry became one of the first people to train nurses in Britain. She herself had worked for many years with women in prison and with very poor people.

Then, Elizabeth set up the Institute of Nursing Sisters. The nurses from the Institute visited the poor in their own homes. They were also sent to Guy's Hospital in London. Here, they were trained to look for signs of disease.

Dorothea Dix was an American woman who came to Britain and saw the work of Elizabeth Fry. She came back to the United States to improve the prisons of Cambridge, Massachusetts. Then, she tried to persuade the state government to build hospitals for mentally ill people. Dorothea had TB. She also caught a disease called **malaria**, which gave her high fevers. Yet, she continued to work. She made it possible for thirty-two new hospitals to be built in the United States.

▶ Elizabeth Fry visits a prison. She learned about the poor and the sick from visits like this one. She also wanted to see how prisoners, the poor, and mentally ill people were treated.

◀ Dorothea Dix was an admirer of Elizabeth Fry's work. She persuaded many states to build hospitals for mentally ill people.

Florence Nightingale

Florence Nightingale is probably the most famous woman in the history of nursing. She was born into a rich family. In those days, the girls in rich families did not work. Florence Nightingale's family was shocked when she went to train as a nurse at the Kaiserwerth training school in Germany.

In 1854, British soldiers were fighting in the Crimean War. Newspaper reports reached London of the "sick suffering soldiers." Florence Nightingale wrote to the British War Office. She said that she wanted to help. A week later, she set out with thirty-eight nurses for Scutari Hospital, near the Black Sea. Her nurses worked hard in the hospital there. Many of the soldiers in the Crimean War were dying of **cholera**.

Florence Nightingale insisted on repairs to the hospital drains. The number of soldiers who died from cholera fell sharply after the repairs were made.

Mary Seacole

Mary Seacole traveled from Jamaica to help the British soldiers during the Crimean War. She opened a rest home for soldiers called the British Hotel. She gave the soldiers food and medicine.

Mary Seacole knew a great deal about medicine although she was not trained as a doctor. One writer said she was as skilful as "the best surgeons." She was also very brave. She did not stay safely in the hospital. She went right out to the battlefield to tend to the soldiers.

▼ This is Florence Nightingale at work in the wards of Scutari Hospital during the Crimean War. The room is heated by a stove. The beds are raised on wooden platforms. The room looks clean and airy.

Special Nursing

In 1860, Florence Nightingale set up a school for nurses in London. The training lasted a year. It was very good training. The nurses even had to learn some Latin so that they could read the labels on medicine bottles. Some doctors said that training nurses was a waste of time. These doctors made Florence very angry.

Today, nurses do not always have the same kind of training. They can choose the type of extra training they may want. Some nurses will be trained to help at births. Some will be trained to take care of people who are mentally ill. Some learn to take care of children or elderly people.

Mental Illness

For hundreds of years, people thought that devils caused mental illness. About 400 years ago, in London, people who had mental illnesses were taken care of in a place called the "house of Bethlehem." The name became shortened to "Bedlam." People were afraid of the patients of Bedlam. They put collars and chains around the patients' necks, so that they could not escape. The money to run Bedlam was raised in a very cruel way. The people were chained up and put on display. Londoners paid a penny to come and see them. No one thought that these people were sick or that an illness of the mind could be cured.

Elizabeth Fry, Dorothea Dix and others worked to set up special hospitals. The doctors and nurses did not know how to cure these people, but they treated them with kindness.

In the late 1880's, a Viennese doctor named Sigmund Freud began to study the minds of people who were mentally ill. He found new ways to help them. This study is called **psychiatry**. Today, nurses are specially trained to treat and care for people who are ill in this way.

Nursing in Wartime

Jean-Henri Dunant from Switzerland was present at a battle during the Crimean War. He was shocked by the suffering of the wounded soldiers. In 1864, he helped to set up the Red Cross Society in Geneva.

An American woman named Clara Barton heard of Dunant's work. During the Civil War, Clara Barton had seen the sufferings of the wounded. She visited Switzerland. On her return to America, she started a Red Cross Society.

Today, Red Cross doctors and nurses still care for wounded soldiers. They travel all over the world to help people who are injured or sick.

◄ Two hundred years ago, people with mental illnesses were feared or laughed at. This is the Bedlam Hospital. One man is being held down with chains. Behind him, in the center, is a man who thinks he is a king. He has been given a crown to make people laugh.

The Red Cross flag is like the Swiss flag with the colors reversed. This is to remember Jean-Henri Dunant, who set up the Red Cross. In Muslim countries, there is a society like the Red Cross. The Muslim sign is a **crescent**, so the society is called the Red Crescent.

▲ Clara Barton learned of the work of the Red Cross in Switzerland and brought the idea to America after the Civil War.

▲ There are Red Cross nurses all over the world. These were nurses of the French Red Cross. They were working with soldiers in Morocco about eighty years ago.

Ears, Eyes, and Teeth

There have been many inventions to help deaf people hear better. Trumpet-shaped devices of all kinds were used to bring sound into the ear. The first hearing aids were animal horns used as ear-trumpets. A king of Portugal who was deaf had a special throne built to help him hear. It had hollow arms with open lions' mouths at the ends. The sound traveled into the lions' mouths, up the arms of the throne to an ear tube.

A hundred years ago, an American named Alexander Graham Bell tried to make a hearing aid. In his effort to make sound travel, he also invented the telephone! In 1923, the Marconi Company began to make hearing aids based on one of Bell's designs. They were too heavy to carry around, however. In 1949, people found out how to make tiny hearing aids. They could be made to fit inside the ear, or behind it.

▲ King João of Portugal was deaf. This special throne helped him to hear better. The hollow arms led to an ear tube.

▼ The man in the center of the painting is testing glasses for himself. He has a large number to choose from. The small boy in front is enjoying himself by trying on glasses, too. His sister does not like them on him.

Eyes

The Romans knew that things look bigger if you see them through water. This is because the water bends the light waves into a bigger picture for the eye. This led to the invention of the **magnifying glass**. This is a piece of glass with a curved surface.

About 700 years ago, people began to put this glass in frames in front of their eyes. We call these **eyeglasses**. By that time, Arab and Persian doctors could already operate on the eyes.

Over 200 years ago, many towns in Europe and North America had stores which sold eyeglasses. A little later, Benjamin Franklin, the American statesman and scientist, had special eyeglasses made. They could help him see in two ways. One half of each glass was for reading. The other was for seeing long distances. They were the first **bifocal** lenses.

Teeth

Five thousand years ago, people in Asia described a toothache as "worms in the teeth." Bad teeth have always been a problem. It was rare in the past to keep your own teeth into old age. People became toothless or had false teeth.

The Etruscans, who lived in Italy 2,500 years ago, made false teeth from human or animal teeth. They were attached to gold rings, which fit over the teeth that were left on each side of the gap left by missing teeth.

From the 1500's onward, you could get a barber to pull out a bad tooth. A French dentist, Pierre Fauchard, became famous in the 1720's. He could fit a false tooth onto the stump of an old one. This was called a **crown**.

President George Washington had a clever dentist named John Greenwood. He made a dentist's drill from his mother's spinning wheel. You can still see the false teeth he made for Washington in the Science Museum in London.

▼ This dentist also works as a barber and as a surgeon. On the outside wall, you can see his striped pole and a street sign, showing blood in a cup. If you look, you will see that his shop is not a very clean place.

Public Health

Ideas about keeping people clean and healthy are not new. Thousands of years ago, the people who lived in the Middle East had many rules about this. The Hebrew people had laws about what to eat and how to keep clean. The Egyptian people had clean, running water in their homes.

The Greeks thought that people should work to keep healthy. They knew that good food and exercise helped people to stay well. The Romans were a practical people. They built pipes to carry clean water to their houses. They also built tunnels to take away dirty water and waste. These were called **sewers**.

When Roman rule in Europe ended about 1,500 years ago, these ideas about public health were forgotten.

▲ A hundred years ago, very few people had water piped into their homes. In this London street, people are collecting it from a pipe running into the street. Cholera and other diseases spread rapidly because of dirty water supplies.

Dirt and Disease

For hundreds of years, people in Europe threw their garbage into the streets. The streets sloped down from the sides to the middle. A channel, or **gutter**, ran down the center of the street. People expected that rain would wash the garbage away. Often, it did not, and the gutter became blocked.

Dogs, horses, and farm animals also dirtied the streets. Rats chewed their way into wooden houses. Waste and dirt were put into large holes called **cesspools**. Often, these cesspools were under the floors of the houses. Diseases spread easily because of this.

◄ The Romans built stone sewers like this one under their cities. The waste-filled water flowed out of the cities and into the rivers.

Little was done to clean up the streets. At this time, people did not know about the link between dirt and disease. They thought that disease was a punishment from God. Also, they thought that bad smells spread diseases. They carried bunches of sweet-smelling herbs and flowers to sniff in the streets. Sometimes, cloves were stuck in an orange. Sometimes, herbs were packed inside round containers called **pomanders**.

Over 200 years ago, many people left the countryside to work in towns and cities. Diseases such as cholera spread easily in the crowded parts of these places. About 72,000 people in Britain died from cholera in 1848.

▼ This boy is getting a vaccination to protect him against tuberculosis. He may have injections to protect him against other diseases, like measles, polio, and tetanus.

Organizing Public Health

The work of Edward Jenner and Louis Pasteur had shown that germs lived in dirt. It also showed that vaccines could stop some diseases from spreading. Many countries started to spend money on public health. In many big cities, like Paris, Rome, London, and New York, underground sewers were built.

Countries started to spend money on providing vaccines for people. Ways of killing germs in the water supply were found. People passed laws to make sure that the food on sale in stores was fit to eat. Other laws were made to keep stores and factories clean.

Today, all countries have laws about public health. Because of this, most diseases do not spread as quickly as they did in the past.

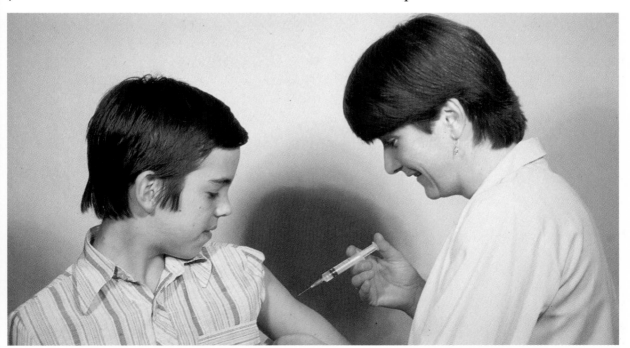

Preventing Disease

Up to a hundred years ago, most public health laws were about clean buildings, food, and water. These laws tried to stop the spread of disease. Sometimes, they seemed very mean. In the 1890's, for example, many families left Europe for America. They sailed in crowded and dirty ships. Often, people became sick with cholera before reaching America.

When the ships arrived in New York harbor, the people were taken to Ellis Island first. There, they were tested by doctors from the United States Public Health Service. A doctor chalked letters on the shoulders of anyone who was not fit to work. L was for lame, M for mentally ill, and so on. Anyone who was sick was sent back to the country he or she came from. The doctors did not want them to be a danger to people in America. Families were split up. Ellis Island became known as "Heartbreak Island."

Improving Health

About eighty years ago, people began to try out new ways to improve public health. They wanted better houses to be built for poor people. The houses had running water and toilets. In some countries, special places called baby clinics were set up. Parents could bring young children to the clinics for vaccinations. The nurses gave advice about how to take care of the children.

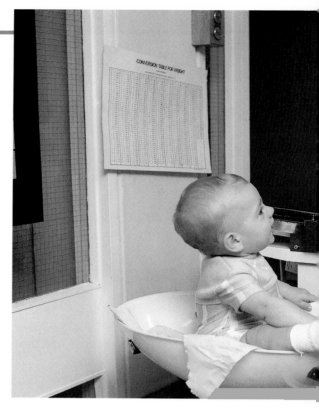

▼ These are children whose families came to settle in America in the 1890's. If they had TB, they were not allowed to enter New York City.

▲ In this health clinic, a baby is being weighed. He will be weighed again in a few weeks to make sure that he is growing properly.

In big countries like the United States and Australia, it was often hard to treat sick people who lived a long way from the hospitals. In 1925, an American nurse named Mary Breckinridge set up the Frontier Service. Her nurses worked in lonely mountain areas of the state of Kentucky. Often, they had to travel on horseback.

In 1928, a flying doctor service was set up in Australia. This service still treats sick patients who live far away from towns or cities. The planes that the service uses are equipped like small hospitals. Very sick patients are flown to larger hospitals.

Other Dangers to Health

Today, many people have never seen anyone with diseases like cholera or TB. They are beginning to forget how dangerous these diseases are. Doctors point out that dangerous diseases of the past can still return.

Travelers in hot countries should also protect themselves against **tropical** diseases. Airports and seaports check people to keep them from bringing animals or plants in from infected countries.

Today, doctors try to teach people to keep healthy. They warn people that some of the things they eat or do could make them sick. For example, eating too much is not good for people, and smoking can cause many diseases, too.

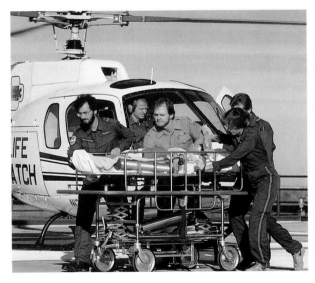

▲ These "flying" doctors are rushing a patient into the hospital. The patient was brought there by helicopter. Flying doctor services like this help to save people in many remote parts of the world.

Medicine Since 1900

Many of the drugs that doctors use today were not known thrity years ago. There are laws to make sure that new drugs are tested before they are used. New vaccines against diseases have been found. Drugs that can kill germs inside the body have also been found. They are called **antibiotics**.

Just over a hundred years ago, scientists began to find out which germs caused which diseases. They also learned how to cure some of them. In 1910, Paul Ehrlich in Germany found a drug called **salvarsan**. This drug was very useful. It could kill germs in the blood without harming the rest of the body. Another name for this drug is 606.

In 1928, Alexander Fleming was carrying out a test with germs in St. Mary's Hospital in London. The lid fell off one of his test dishes. A hairy fur called **mold** started to grow in this dish. At first, Fleming thought that his test had been ruined. Then, he saw that the germs in the dish did not grow near this mold. He had found a drug called **penicillin**. Penicillin can kill many kinds of germs. It was ten years before doctors found a way to make enough of this drug to give it to patients.

▼ Alexander Fleming discovered penicillin in 1928. Two other doctors, Howard Florey and Ernst Chain, developed it as an antibiotic. All three won a Nobel Prize in 1945 for their work.

Seeing inside the Body

In 1895, a German professor, named Wilhelm Roëntgen, found out about **X-rays**. These are light rays that can pass through the body. He used X-rays to take photographs of the inside of the body. This led to the use of the X-ray machine.

Some years later, Marie and Pierre Curie discovered a powerful metal. It was called **radium**. It can be used to treat growths in the body. The Curies did not know that too much radium burns into the body. Marie Curie died of radium burns, but later her discovery helped to save many lives.

Today, there are new machines called **CAT-scans**. These link X-ray machines with computers. They can take very clear pictures of the inside of the body. Since the 1970's, CAT-scans have helped in the fight against many diseases.

▲ Pierre and Marie Curie worked for four years in a cold laboratory with a leaking roof before they first made radium. Marie Curie became the first woman professor of physics in Paris. She won a Nobel Prize for physics in 1903 and one for chemistry in 1911.

Diet and Disease

Sailors have known for many years that lemon or lime juice can prevent a disease called scurvy. For hundreds of years, no one knew why.

In 1913, Casimir Funk of the University of Wisconsin found out that food contains many things that are needed for a healthy body. These are called **vitamins**. Later, a British scientist, named Frederick Gowland Hopkins, showed that many diseases were caused because people did not eat the right kind of food.

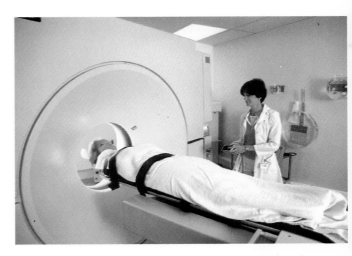

▲ This is a CAT-scan machine. It uses a circle of X-rays to make a picture of a "layer" of the body. Doctors can use this picture to see what is wrong with the patient.

Medicine in the Future

In the last forty years, there have been many new discoveries. In 1953, an American scientist named James Watson, and a British scientist named Francis Crick were working together. They found out what happens in the smallest parts, or **cells**, of the body. This has led to new knowledge about the way that diseases can be passed on from parents to their children.

Cancer

A cancer is a group of living cells that begins to grow out of control. No one knows yet exactly why this happens. Doctors have found some treatments to help control the disease. As yet, there is no cure, but scientists are trying hard to find one.

Computers and Machines

Today, it is possible to make a faulty heart pump properly. Surgeons put a small machine called a **pacemaker** into the chest to help to control the heartbeat. In the future, machines of this kind may be too small to see with the naked eye. It may be possible to link these tiny machines to computers. They will be able to show doctors what is happening in the body. New machines may be able to warn doctors of diseases as soon as they begin. Then people can be treated quickly before the disease spreads.

▼ This woman is being treated for cancer with radiation. The radiation helps to kill the cancer cells. The radiation treatment has to be used very carefully, or the woman could become sick from it.

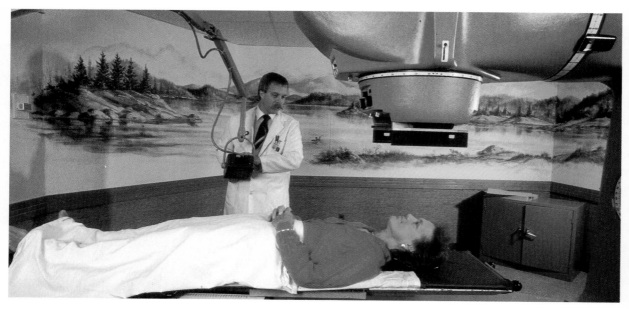

Transplants

In recent years, surgeons have found a way to repair the body by putting in new parts. Some of these like hip joints can be made out of plastic. Other parts, like hearts and lungs, can at present only come from other people. This is called **transplant** surgery. Christiaan Barnard became the first surgeon to transplant a heart, in 1967. In the future, it may be possible to replace many parts of the body. Will people have hearts, lungs, or kidneys that have been made in factories?

Looking Back

Today, some doctors are studying other forms of medicine. They are looking at medicines and treatments that are used in other parts of the world or were used long ago. They are finding that some methods like acupuncture or herbal medicines can still help. They are even beginning, in special cases, to use leeches again to help treat diseases of the blood.

Many people think that medicine in some countries only treats the effects of a disease instead of treating the causes. Sometimes, people are sick because they do not eat the right food. Sometimes, they make themselves sick by worrying about their problems. These sicknesses cannot be cured by medicines. Other people are looking at the whole way in which people live. They suggest changes in lifestyles which may help people to stay healthy. Perhaps the cures of the future will be found by looking back at the past.

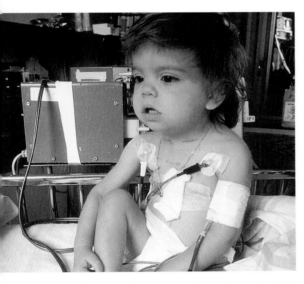

▲ When the kidneys do not work as they should, poisons get into the blood. This child is having her blood cleaned by a kidney machine. She may have to have this done two or three times a week. If she could have a kidney transplant, she would no longer need the treatment.

▶ Today, the Chinese treatment called acupuncture is being used in many parts of the world. Needles are put in special parts of the body. This patient is having acupuncture and electrical treatment together.

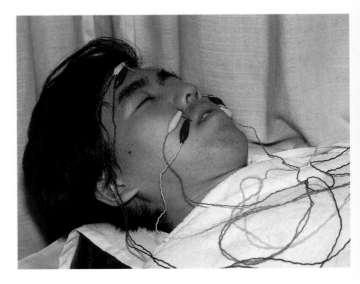

Quiz

How much can you remember? Try this quiz. Use the glossary and the index to help you check your answers.

1. Here are some types of diseases with the letters scrambled. Unscramble them to find the correct names.

    a) IALRMAA, b) LMALSOXP, c) YOELPRS, d) HELORAC

2. Complete the following sentences with (a), (b), (c) or (d):

    1) Who discovered penicillin?
       a) William Harvey
       b) Alexandra Palace
       c) Alexander Fleming
       d) Marie Curie

    2) During which war did Florence Nightingale nurse soldiers?
       a) The Crimean War
       b) The Second World War
       c) The Crusades
       d) The Civil War

    3) For what is Louis Pasteur best known?
       a) Discovering radium
       b) Discovering the microscope
       c) Discovering the milkshake
       d) Discovering germs

    4) Who did the first heart transplant operation in 1967?
       a) Dr. Barnardo
       b) Dr. Watson
       c) Dr. Crippen
       d) Dr. Barnard

    5) Wilhelm Roëntgen made an important discovery. What was it?
       a) The BCG vaccine
       b) The X-ray
       c) The TB germ
       d) Television

    6) What is a CAT–scan?
       a) A machine for hearing the heart beat
       b) A machine for cleaning the blood
       c) A machine for examining animals
       d) A machine for seeing inside the body

3. Who
    a) treated the wounds of soldiers and made an artificial hand for one of them?
    b) fell asleep under a table?
    c) was one of the first women to train as a doctor in the United States?
    d) died of radium burns?

4. Why are these people famous?
    a) William Harvey
    b) Joseph Lister
    c) Father Damien
    d) Franz Mesmer

5. Match the descriptions given in (a) to (f) with the words numbered in (1) to (6) below.

    a) Used to cover a wound
    b) A disease carried by rats
    c) A hospital in the Crimea in Russia
    d) A disease carried by cows
    e) Used to see very small objects
    f) A hospital for mentally ill people, in London

    1) Bedlam
    2) a microscope
    3) the plague

4) a bandage
5) Scutari
6) tuberculosis

6. These words begin with the same letter. They are written backwards. Figure out what each word says and give its meaning.
a) RETEMOMREHT, b) TNALPSNART,
c) GNINNAPERT

7. Which of these statements is True or False?
a) The sign of medicine is a tree with a plant around it.
b) Mary Seacole nursed soldiers in the Crimean War.
c) People who pretended to be doctors were called ducks.
d) If you have had cowpox, you will not catch smallpox.
e) People used to go to the butcher to have their teeth pulled out.

8. Put the following events in the order in which they took place.
a) Nursing monks in Jerusalem looked after Christian travelers.
b) Pacemakers were invented.
c) Clara Barton began the American Red Cross.
d) Pierre Fauchard invented a false tooth to fit over an old tooth.
e) Small hearing aids were invented.

9. Which word does not belong to each group?
a) ether, chloroform, nitrous oxide, thermometer
b) malaria, scurvy, pomanders, tuberculosis
c) eyeglasses, bifocals, bicycle, magnifying glass
d) mumps, salvarsan, penicillin, opium

ANSWERS

1. a) MALARIA b) SMALLPOX c) LEPROSY
   d) CHOLERA
2. (1) c, (2) a, (3) d, (4) d, (5) b, (6) d
3. a) Ambroise Paré
   b) James Simpson
   c) Elizabeth Blackwell
   d) Marie Curie
4. a) He discovered how the heart works.
   b) He showed how to keep germs from wounds.
   c) He helped lepers.
   d) He invented hypnosis.
5. (a) 4, (b) 3, (c) 5, (d) 6, (e) 2, (f) 1
6. a) thermometer – used to measure temperature
   b) transplant – operation to put new parts in the body
   c) trepanning – operation to make an opening in the skull
7. a) false, b) true, c) false, d) true, e) false
8. (a), (d), (c), (e), (b)
9. a) thermometer (all the others put people to sleep)
   b) pomanders (all the others are diseases)
   c) bicycle (all the others help you to see better)
   d) mumps (all the others are drugs)

45

Glossary

acupuncture: a Chinese method of curing sickness by sticking needles into special places on the body.

amputate: to cut off part of or whole of an arm or leg.

anaesthetic: something that makes people or animals lose their sense of pain.

antibiotic: a special type of chemical that can kill germs. It is a medicine.

apothecary: a person who makes medicines; a druggist.

artery: a tube in the body that carries fresh blood to the body.

bifocals: eyeglasses where each glass has two parts. One part is for nearsightedness and the other is for farsightedness.

bile: a thick, sour liquid made by the liver.

bowel: the tubes inside the body, below the stomach, that carry waste matter.

Caesarean section: an operation used to help a mother give birth.

capillaries: the very tiny tubes which connect arteries to veins.

carbolic acid: a strong liquid which kills germs.

CAT-scan: a machine that takes photographs of the inside of a body.

cell: the smallest part that makes up any living thing.

cesspool: a large, underground hole. It is used to collect waste drainage from houses.

chloroform: a colorless liquid with a strong, sweet smell. If you breathe it in, it can put you to sleep.

cholera: a disease which gives people very bad diarrhea and vomiting. Cholera is spread by unclean water and food.

cowpox: a disease that humans can catch from cows.

crescent: a curved shape, like a new moon.

crown: the part of the tooth you can see, or a new false tooth that covers an old, broken one.

disease: a serious sickness.

dissect: to cut something open so the insides can be looked at.

epidemic: a disease that spreads easily and rapidly from one person or animal to another.

ether: a colorless liquid with a special smell. When you breathe it in, it can put you to sleep.

eyeglasses: two pieces of glass (lenses) held in a frame in front of the eyes, which improve eyesight.

germ: a tiny living thing which can multiply and spread disease.

gutter: a drain which carries off rainwater and waste.

Hebrew: (1) a Jewish person from Israel. (2) the Jewish language.

herb: (1) any plant that does not have a woody stalk and completely dies each year. (2) any plant used for medicine or to add flavor to food.

Hippocratic oath: a statement made by new doctors in which they promise to follow a set of rules about treating their patients.

hospitality: the friendly welcoming of guests and strangers.

humor: (1) one of the four fluids of the body which long ago were thought to affect health.

hypnosis: a false type of sleep where the mind is still awake.

laboratory: a building or room where scientists work on experiments.

leech: a blood-sucking worm.

leprosy: a serious, usually fatal, disease of the skin and nerves.

magnifying glass: a piece of glass that makes things look larger.

malaria: a dangerous disease carried by certain mosquitoes.

miasma: an unpleasant smell.

microbe: a very small living thing that causes disease.

microscope: an instrument that makes very small things look bigger.

midwife: a woman who helps with the birth of a baby.

mold: a woolly growth found on food that has gone bad.

natural: something that exists in the world around us.

nitrous oxide: a strong gas that when breathed in puts people to sleep or makes them laugh.

opium: a powder made from a special poppy. It is a strong drug.

pacemaker: an electronic machine which keeps the heart beating steadily.

pasteurize: a way of heating milk which kills all the germs.

penicillin: a drug or chemical made from mold which kills many sorts of germs.

Persia: the old name for the country of Iran.

pharmacist: a person who has been trained to make medicines.

phlegm: a thick, slimy substance made in the throat.

plague: a deadly disease that is spread very quickly. It is carried by rats and fleas.

pomander: a ball which holds perfumes and which has holes through which the smell escapes.

prescription: a written note from a doctor stating the medicines needed by a patient.

psychiatry: the study of the mind.

radium: a metal found in minerals that can cure some diseases. It is radioactive.

salvarsan: a strong drug which is now rarely used.

science: the study of something by watching, testing, and experimenting.

scurvy: a disease caused by the lack of vitamin C.

sepsis: when germs get into a cut and infect the body.

sewer: a pipe that carries away water and waste. It is usually built underground.

shock: the dangerous reaction of the body to pain.

smallpox: a disease that caused high fever and many blisters. People very often died from it, or were badly scarred.

surgeon: a person who treats diseases and injuries by operating on the body.

transplant: an operation in which something is removed from one person's body and put into someone else's body.

trepanning: an ancient operation in which an opening is made in the skull.

tropical: describes something to do with, or from, the tropics. The tropics are hot, damp parts of the world near the Equator.

tuberculosis: a serious, infectious disease of the lungs.

vaccination: an injection of a substance that protects a person from catching a disease.

vein: a tube in the body which carries used blood back to the heart.

vitamin: a substance which is found in foods such as vegetables and fruit. Vitamins are essential for good health.

X-ray: a light ray which can be used to photograph the insides of a body.

Index